GW00360204

LA DIGUE TRAVEL GUIDE 2023

La Digue's Best Beaches and Where to Find
Them

Sheila J. Ryder

Copyright©2023 Sheila J. Ryder

AllRightsReserved.

Table of content

Introduction

Welcome to the La Digue Beach Travel Guide, where we take you on a journey through one of the most breathtaking islands in the Seychelles. La Digue is a place where you can escape the hustle and bustle of everyday life and immerse yourself in its natural beauty.

This guidebook has been crafted for all types of travelers, whether you are looking for a romantic getaway, a family vacation, or an adventurous trip filled with hiking and water sports. With our expertise and insider tips, you will be able to make the most out of your stay in La Digue.

Our guidebook is filled with factual information about La Digue, including its history, geological background, and cultural significance. We also provide detailed information about the island's main attractions, including its stunning beaches, lush forests, and unique wildlife.

Our guidebook also covers practical considerations, such as the best time to visit, how to get around the island, and where to find the best accommodations and restaurants.

We have also included helpful tips and advice on how to stay safe, respect local customs, and ensure that you leave no trace on this beautiful island.

Whether you are a seasoned traveler or a first-time visitor to the Seychelles, the La Digue Beach Travel Guide is the perfect companion to help you make the most of your trip. So, sit back, relax, and let us take you on a journey through one of the most enchanting islands in the world.

Why visit La Digue Island

La Digue Island is an idyllic tropical paradise located in the Seychelles. With its unspoiled beaches, crystal clear waters, and lush natural landscape, La Digue is a must-visit destination for any traveler seeking an unforgettable experience. Here are some reasons why you should visit La Digue Island:

1. The beaches: La Digue has some of the most beautiful beaches in the world. Anse Source d'Argent is the most famous of them, with its towering granite boulders, white sand beach, and shallow turquoise waters. Another must-visit is Anse Coco, which is accessible only by foot and offers a secluded and peaceful alternative to the more popular beaches.

2. The natural beauty: La Digue is home to a truly unique natural environment, with

granite rock formations, lush forests, and a variety of exotic flora and fauna. The island is surrounded by a coral reef teeming with marine life, and visitors can also explore the nearby nature reserves, such as Veuve Reserve and the Union Estate Park.

3. The culture: La Digue Island has a rich cultural heritage, with a mix of African, Asian, and European influences. Visitors can learn about the island's history at the La Digue Island Heritage Village and explore the traditional Creole architecture and lifestyle.

4. The adventure: La Digue Island offers a range of outdoor activities, from hiking and cycling to snorkeling and scuba diving. The island's waters are known for their clear visibility and diverse marine life, and visitors can explore the many wreck sites and shallow reefs.

5. The relaxation: La Digue is the perfect destination for those seeking a peaceful and relaxing getaway. With its laid-back island vibes, pristine beaches, and gorgeous scenery, it's the ideal place to unwind and recharge.

In conclusion, La Digue Island is an unforgettable travel destination that offers something for everyone. Whether you're seeking adventure, relaxation, or simply a break from the hustle and bustle of everyday life, La Digue Island is a must-visit destination that will leave you with memories to last a lifetime.

Brief history and culture of La Digue

La Digue Island, located in the Seychelles, has a rich cultural and historical heritage that makes it an exciting destination for travelers interested in learning more about the region's past. Here's a brief overview of the history and culture of La Digue:

History:

La Digue Island was first discovered by French explorers in the 18th century and was later annexed by the British in 1811. The island's economy was based on coconut farming, which was introduced in the mid-1800s and continued to thrive until the early 20th century. The coconut industry was replaced by vanilla production, which became the island's primary source of income until tourism emerged in the mid-20th century.

Culture:

La Digue Island is home to a diverse mix of cultures, including African, Asian, and European influences. The island's population is largely Creole, which is a blend of African, European, and Malagasy heritage. The island's culture is reflected in its architecture, cuisine, music, and festivals.

Architecture:

The traditional Creole architecture of La Digue is characterized by colorful wooden houses with steep roofs and verandas. These buildings are made of locally sourced materials and are designed to withstand the island's tropical climate. Visitors can explore the island's architecture at the La Digue Island Heritage Village, which is home to historic houses, a cemetery, and a museum.

Cuisine:

La Digue Island's cuisine is a mixture of local and international flavors. The island's seafood is particularly famous, with grilled fish, octopus curry, and shark chutney being popular dishes. Visitors can also sample locally grown fruits and vegetables, such as breadfruit, coconuts, and mangoes.

Music and Festivals:

Music is an important part of La Digue Island's culture, with traditional Creole music still being performed at festivals throughout the year. The island's most famous festival is the Feast of Assumption, which takes place in August and features music, dancing, and religious ceremonies.

In conclusion, La Digue Island's history and culture are an important part of what makes this destination unique. Visitors can explore the island's architecture, cuisine, and festivals to gain insight into the region's past and present.

An Overview of La Digue's Beaches

La Digue's beaches offer a unique and unforgettable experience for visitors. In this guide , we will provide an overview of La Digue's beaches, highlighting their individual characteristics and features.

1. Anse Source D'Argent

Anse Source D'Argent is perhaps the most famous beach in La Digue, and for good reason. With its natural rock formations, white sand, and crystal-clear waters, it's easy to see why. Visitors can explore the many coves and lagoons that make up the beach, as well as the nearby coconut groves and plantations. It's best to visit Anse Source D'Argent during low tide to fully appreciate all it has to offer.

2. Anse Marron

For those seeking a more secluded and adventurous beach experience, Anse Marron is the perfect destination. The beach can only be reached by a challenging hike that winds through the jungle, up steep cliffs, and over boulders. However, the reward at the end is well worth it. Anse Marron is a hidden gem with pristine sand and turquoise waters, making it one of the most picturesque beaches on the island.

3. Grande Anse

Grande Anse is La Digue's longest beach, stretching for over a kilometer along the island's eastern coast. The beach is famous for its powdery white sand and crystal-clear waters, making it an ideal spot for swimming, sunbathing, and snorkeling. Visitors can explore the nearby lush vegetation and breathtaking views of the coastline.

4. Petite Anse

Located near Anse Cocos and accessible only on foot or by boat, Petite Anse is another secluded and picturesque beach on La Digue. The beach is a popular spot for snorkeling and swimming, and visitors can observe marine life such as turtles and colorful fish.

5. Anse Cocos

Anse Cocos is another secluded beach that can only be accessed by foot or by boat. The hike to the beach takes visitors through lush vegetation and over rocky terrain, but the destination is worth the effort. Anse Cocos is surrounded by granite boulders, and the waves are perfect for swimming and bodyboarding.

In conclusion, La Digue's beaches are among the most beautiful in the world, with each offering a unique and unforgettable experience to visitors. Whether you're seeking a secluded spot or a long beach for sunbathing, La Digue has a beach that will meet your needs. However, visitors should always be respectful of the environment and follow local guidelines to preserve the natural beauty of the island.

What makes La Digue beaches unique

There are several reasons that make La Digue beaches unique, and these factors have contributed to the island's popularity as a world-class tourist destination. In this guide, we will delve into what makes La Digue beaches unique and explore the reasons why visitors from all over the world flock to this paradise.

Granite Boulders

One feature that sets La Digue beaches apart from others is the presence of granite boulders. These magnificent rocks are a unique feature of the island's geography and can be seen at Anse Source D'Argent, one of the island's most famous beaches.

The granite boulders form a stunning backdrop against the clear blue waters and soft white sands, creating an unforgettable and picturesque scene. Visitors love to take photographs with these natural sculptures, which provide a unique and artistic touch to the beach.

Stunning Natural Landscapes

La Digue is a visually stunning island that boasts of natural beauty that has remained untouched by human impact. The beaches are surrounded by lush green vegetation, which provides a natural canopy that shades visitors from the sun. The tropical forests of the island create a scenic backdrop that enhances the beauty of the beaches.

Visitors can explore the areas around the beach and enjoy the lush greenery, which is home to a wide range of exotic wildlife. The island is also home to several nature reserves and parks, where visitors can take guided tours and enjoy close encounters with the island's flora and fauna.

The Calm and Tranquil Waters

The waters surrounding La Digue's beaches are calm and tranquil, creating a serene environment that's perfect for swimming, snorkeling, and other marine activities. The water is also clear, providing a clear view of the coral reefs and the colorful fish that swim in the waters.

The warm waters are ideal for visitors who want to enjoy a swim and relax their bodies and minds. The beaches provide a perfect getaway from the hustle and bustle of daily life, and visitors can enjoy the peaceful surroundings without disturbance.

Authentic Island Experience

La Digue is a unique destination that offers a real island experience to visitors. The island is not overcrowded with the touristy vibe, unlike some other beach destinations. The laid-back lifestyle on the island is a welcome change that visitors appreciate, and it allows them to connect more deeply with the local culture.

The island is small enough to explore on foot, and visitors can interact with the locals, who are friendly and welcoming to tourists. This allows visitors to experience the authentic lifestyle of the people of the island.

Conclusion

La Digue's beaches offer visitors a chance to experience natural beauty and tranquility that's unparalleled to any other beach destination. The unique combination of granite boulders, stunning natural landscapes, clear waters, and the authentic island experience makes La Digue's beaches truly unique.

Visitors to the island are captivated by the beauty of the island, the richness of the culture, and the warmth of the people. La Digue is an ideal destination for tourists who seek to escape the stresses of daily life and want to indulge in the natural beauty that the world has to offer.

Best time of the year to visit La Digue beaches

If you're planning a visit to La Digue beaches, you must know the best time of the year to experience the best weather and avoid seasonal crowds. In this guide, we will explore the best time of the year to visit La Digue beaches and get the most out of your island getaway.

High Season: May to September

The best time to visit La Digue's beaches is during the high season, which lasts from May to September. During this time, the weather is dry and sunny, giving visitors the perfect opportunity to enjoy the beaches' warm tropical climate. The temperatures during the day are high, ranging from 28°C to 30°C, and the nights are cooler with temperatures averaging around 24°C to 26°C.

The water temperature remains warm during this time, making it ideal for swimming, snorkeling, and other water activities. The absence of wind and rough seas offer visitors calm and tranquil waters to relax in and enjoy their beach vacation freely.

Another benefit of visiting during the high season is, there are lesser crowds than at other times of the year. Visitors can enjoy the beaches more peacefully, with plenty of opportunities to book local accommodations and activities.

Shoulder Season: October to April

The shoulder season, which ranges from October to April, is also an excellent time to visit La Digue's beaches. The temperatures during this time are warmer than during the high season, with day temperatures at an average of 30°C to 33°C, and night temperatures range from 26°C to 28°C.

During this time, humidity levels are higher and sporadic rainfall is expected. However, the good thing is, the rainfall is light and brief, and visitors can still enjoy the beach activities during the sunny hours of the day. The clear and sunny weather can spread for several weeks at a time, allowing visitors to enjoy their vacation to the fullest.

One thing to keep in mind when visiting during the shoulder season is to be prepared for the high demand for tourist accommodations. Many visitors, especially around the Christmas and New Year holidays, book in advance, resulting in limited spaces. Ensure to plan well to get the best deals and reservations during your stay.

Low Season: May to September

The low season in La Digue, which is typically from May to September, is the time of the year to avoid if you're planning to visit the island to enjoy the beaches. The weather is characterized by the monsoon season, bringing heavier, longer, and more frequent rainfall. Wind can also make the beaches uncomfortable and rough.

However, the prices during this time are lower, making it an attractive period for budget travelers. For those that want to experience the culture and lifestyle of the locals or wish to engage in other land activities like trekking, the low season can be perfect.

Conclusion

La Digue beaches offer breathtaking views and tropical climate all around the year. The best time to visit the beaches is during the high season, from May to September, providing visitors with sunny and dry weather, warm waters, and with fewer crowds. The shoulder season from October to April can also be ideal when well prepared for sporadic rains. Still, visitors can enjoy lower prices and adequate availability of reservations. It is, however, crucial to avoid the low season from May to September due to poor weather conditions and rough seas.

Anse Source d'Argent Beach

Anse Source d'Argent Beach is one of the well-known and picturesque beaches located on the southern coast of La Digue Island, Seychelles. It is a destination that attracts visitors from all around the world because of its unique and breathtaking features, which include towering granite boulders, soft powdery white sand, and crystal-clear shallow waters.

The beach, which is often regarded as one of the world's most beautiful beaches, stretches for over a kilometer and is characterized by a series of coves and inlets that offer visitors various options for exploration and relaxation. The shallow and calm waters make Anse Source d'Argent Beach an ideal spot for swimming, paddling, and other water activities, especially for children.

One of the features that make Anse Source d'Argent Beach stand out is its unique and surreal blend of granite boulders weathered over time into fantastic shapes and curves by wind and water. These granite boulders not only add to the beach's beauty but also provide sheltered areas and shaded spots for visitors to relax and soak in the spectacular views.

The soft, powdery white sand of Anse Source d'Argent Beach is another of its fantastic features, which extends for over a kilometer, and is soft and comfortable for barefoot walking, sunbathing, or picnicking. The sand is also cool to the touch, making it an ideal spot for relaxation and unwinding.

The beach is also surrounded by lush greenery and tropical vegetation, which provides a refreshing and cool environment, especially during the hot afternoons. The lush vegetation is home to plenty of flora and fauna, which visitors can explore while on nature walks, hikes, or cycling tours.

The beach is easily accessible, and visitors can enjoy a range of activities offered here, such as snorkeling, scuba diving, paddleboarding, kayaking, and jet skiing. They can also indulge in beachside barbecues and parties or enjoy a stroll on the beach, taking in the views, and watching the sunset.

Another feature of Anse Source d'Argent Beach is the presence of a coral reef, which is home to a variety of marine life, including tropical fish, octopus, and sea turtles. Visitors can join guided snorkeling or diving tours to explore the reef and get up close to the colorful marine life.

Facilities at Anse Source d'Argent Beach include picnic tables, beach chairs, umbrellas, showers, restrooms, and food vendors. They also provide water sports equipment for hire, such as snorkeling gear, kayaks, and paddleboards.

In conclusion, Anse Source d'Argent Beach is a destination that offers awe-inspiring views, unique geological features, and a range of activities that cater to all ages and interests. It is a must-visit destination for any traveler to La Digue island, Seychelles, seeking to experience a tropical paradise with outstanding natural beauty.

Grand Anse Beach

Grand Anse Beach is one of the most beautiful and unspoiled beaches in La Digue, Seychelles. Located on the island's southern coast, this stunning crescent-shaped beach stretches for almost one and a half kilometers, offering visitors a tranquil and serene escape from the hustle and bustle of the modern world.

The beach boasts of its picturesque setting, with crystal-clear turquoise waters, soft white sand, and lush palm trees. Unlike many other beaches in the area, Grand Anse Beach remains relatively untouched, with no major resorts or high-rise buildings dominating the surrounding area.

The beach is situated in a secluded bay that is entirely surrounded by granite cliffs and dense vegetation, making it the perfect place to unwind, relax and enjoy the tranquillity of the surroundings. The calm and shallow waters are perfect for swimming, paddling, and snorkelling, although care should be taken when entering the water due to the presence of strong currents.

One of the most striking features of Grand Anse Beach is the enormous granite boulders strewn along the coast, which provide a dramatic contrast with the turquoise waters. These giant boulders form natural pools, tide pools, and coves that are perfect for intimate relaxation and sunbathing.

Another unique feature of Grand Anse Beach is the diverse marine life that inhabits the area. Visitors can see a variety of tropical fish, starfish, sea turtles, and other marine creatures visible in the crystal-clear waters. Snorkelling and diving are popular activities among tourists seeking to see the underwater world.

Visitors to Grand Anse Beach can also enjoy a range of activities, such as cycling, hiking, and birdwatching in the surrounding area. The beach is easily accessible by bus, bike, or foot, and there is ample parking for those with private cars.

The nearby shops, cafes, and takeaways offer visitors a variety of cuisines, refreshments and snacks. Picnic tables and shaded areas are also available for those wishing to host their own beach barbecues.

In conclusion, Grand Anse Beach is a hidden gem in the Seychelles that offers a picture-perfect setting with spectacular views, a wide range of activities, and unparalleled tranquillity. It is a must-visit destination for any traveler seeking to explore La Digue island's natural beauty.

Coco Beach Anse

Coco Beach Anse is a picturesque and secluded beach located on the east coast of Mahe Island, Seychelles. The beach is situated in a small cove that is surrounded by lush tropical flora, creating a peaceful and tranquil environment for visitors.

Coco Beach Anse is renowned for its crystal-clear turquoise waters, soft white sand, and striking granite boulders that are scattered along the coastline. The beach is relatively small, providing an intimate and secluded experience for visitors seeking a private and peaceful haven.

One of the most unique features of Coco Beach Anse is the stunning granite boulders that are scattered along the coast. These boulders form natural tide pools, which are perfect for swimming and bathing in, and provide visitors with a unique and memorable experience.

Another feature of Coco Beach Anse that sets it apart from other beaches in the Seychelles is the diversity of marine life that can be found in the area. Snorkelling and diving are popular activities among visitors who wish to explore the underwater world and see a host of exotic marine creatures, including colorful tropical fish, sea turtles, and even dolphins.

Coco Beach Anse is not just known for its natural beauty; visitors can also enjoy a range of recreational activities, such as beach volleyball, paddleboarding, kayaking and various water sports. The beach offers ample space for cycling, jogging or simply taking a leisurely stroll along its shores.

The beach is also a popular spot for picnics, with numerous BBQ pits and picnic tables available for visitors to relax and enjoy a meal with their loved ones while taking in the stunning views.

For those who prefer a bit of solitude, there are plenty of shaded areas where visitors can relax, unwind and soak up the peace and quiet. The surrounding fauna and flora provide a stunning natural backdrop, creating a sense of tranquillity and serenity that is hard to find anywhere else.

Coco Beach Anse is easily accessible by bus or taxi, and ample parking is available for those who prefer to travel by car. There are several food shacks and restaurants nearby, offering a range of cuisines, refreshments and snacks.

In conclusion, Coco Beach Anse is a hidden

gem in the Seychelles that offers a unique and intimate beach experience unlike any other. Its stunning natural beauty, coupled with the variety of activities and recreational areas, makes it an ideal destination for couples, families, and solo travelers who are looking for a peaceful and secluded escape.

Beach Activities and Tours

Beaches are a popular destination for travelers seeking some fun in the sun and relaxation. However, beaches offer much more than just swimming and sunbathing. With a range of beach activities and tours available, visitors can take their beach experience to the next level and explore all that the area has to offer.

One popular beach activity is snorkeling. Snorkeling is a fantastic way to explore the underwater world and see a range of marine creatures up close. With a mask and snorkel, visitors can venture into the water and swim alongside colorful fish, sea turtles, and even dolphins. Many beaches offer equipment rental or guided tours for visitors who want to try snorkeling but don't have their own gear or experience.

Another popular beach activity is surfing. With waves of varying sizes and intensities, surfing is a thrilling sport that requires skill, balance, and courage. Beaches with strong waves and consistent surf conditions are ideal for surfing, and many offer surf lessons for beginners. Advanced surfers can rent boards and hit the waves on their own, while beginners can take advantage of the guidance of a professional instructor.

Kayaking and paddleboarding are also popular beach activities. These activities allow visitors to explore the coast and get a different perspective of the surrounding scenery. With calm waters, kayaking and paddleboarding are easy and enjoyable for all skill levels. Many beaches offer equipment rental or guided tours, allowing visitors to explore on their own or with a group.

Beach volleyball is a popular social activity that is enjoyed by visitors of all ages. With a net and ball, visitors can set up their own game or join in on a game with others. Beach volleyball is a fun way to get some exercise, socialize with other visitors, and enjoy the beautiful beach surroundings.

For visitors who want to explore beyond the beach, there are a variety of tours and activities available. Island-hopping tours provide visitors with the opportunity to explore the surrounding islands and learn about the local culture and history. Many beaches also offer guided hikes and nature walks that allow visitors to explore the natural beauty of the area.

Fishing tours are another popular activity for visitors who want to experience the local fishing industry and catch their own dinner.

Visitors can join a guided fishing tour or rent their own equipment and explore the waters on their own.

In conclusion, beaches offer much more than just swimming and sunbathing. With a range of beach activities and tours available, visitors can take their beach experience to the next level and explore all that the area has to offer. Whether it's snorkeling, surfing, kayaking, beach volleyball or island-hopping tours, there is something for everyone at the beach.

Beach Picnics and Barbecues

Beach picnics and barbecues are a popular pastime for families, friends and couples to enjoy the sun and the sand while indulging in a scrumptious meal. With the sound of crashing waves in the background and a warm sea breeze blowing, eating at the beach not only allows you to soak up some much-needed vitamin D but also offers a wonderful view.

When planning a beach picnic or barbecue, there are a few key things to consider. First and foremost, check if there are any regulations or rules regarding outdoor cooking at the beach. In some areas, barbecues may not be allowed, or there may be specific fire regulations to follow. Check with local authorities or park rangers for guidance before starting your fire or setting up your grill.

Once you have checked on the rules, the next step is to decide on the menu. Many people opt for foods that are easy to prepare and transport, such as sandwiches, chips, fruit, and salads. Grilling at the beach is also a popular option, where you can cook up burgers, hot dogs, seafood, and vegetables. It's best to pre-marinate your meats and pack them in a cooler with plenty of ice to keep them fresh.

When setting up for your beach picnic or barbecue, make sure to bring a large blanket or groundsheet to put your food on. This keeps the sand and dirt from getting on your food and provides a comfortable spot to sit. It's also a good idea to bring a large umbrella or tent to provide shade and shelter from the sun or unexpected rain.

Another important factor to consider when planning a beach picnic or barbecue is safety. Always bring a fire extinguisher or bucket of water to extinguish any stray flames. Keep a close eye on children and pets to ensure that they do not get too close to the fire or grill.

When it comes to cleaning up after your beach picnic or barbecue, be sure to collect and dispose of all trash properly. Never leave food behind, as this can attract unwanted wildlife. Pack up your barbecue or dispose of the coals in a designated area away from any vegetation or nearby structures.

In conclusion, beach picnics and barbecues are a great way to spend time with loved ones and enjoy the beautiful surroundings while indulging in a delicious meal. By following some simple guidelines and safety precautions, you can ensure a fun and memorable beach picnic or barbecue experience. Be sure to check local regulations, plan the menu, bring appropriate equipment and supplies, and don't forget to clean up afterward.

Where to Stay in La Digue

With a limited number of accommodation options, choosing where to stay in La Digue can be a challenging task. In this guide, we will discuss some of the best places to stay in La Digue, based on budget, location, and amenities.

Budget-friendly accommodation:

If you are looking for budget-friendly accommodation, guesthouses and small hotels are the best options in La Digue. These accommodations offer simple yet comfortable rooms at affordable rates. Some of the best budget-friendly accommodations in La Digue are:

• **Chez Marston Guest House:** Located close to the beach, this guesthouse offers spacious rooms, a garden, and a terrace at an affordable price.

• **Buisson Guesthouse:** Located in a quiet neighborhood, this guesthouse provides cozy rooms at a budget-friendly price.

• **Casa De Leela Guesthouse:** Offering a peaceful environment, this guesthouse provides simple but comfortable rooms with a garden terrace.

Mid-range accommodation:

For those who prefer more amenities and comfort, La Digue has a range of mid-range accommodations to choose from. These accommodations typically offer more extensive services and facilities, such as swimming pools, restaurants, and spas. Some of the best mid-range accommodations in La Digue are:

- **Le Relax Beach Resort:** Located on the Anse Reunion beach, this resort provides comfortable rooms, a pool, and a restaurant.

- **Patatran Village Hotel:** Situated on the picturesque Anse Patates beach, this hotel provides comfortable rooms, a pool, and a beachside bar.

- **Le Domaine de L'Orangeraie:** This luxury resort offers spacious villas, a spa, infinity pool, and an excellent restaurant.

Luxury accommodation:

For those seeking an indulgent and sophisticated experience, La Digue has some of the finest luxury accommodation options in Seychelles. These accommodations offer lavish facilities and amenities, such as private beaches, infinity pools, exquisite dining experiences, and spa treatments. Some of the best luxury accommodations in La Digue are:

• **Patatran Village Hotel:** Situated on the picturesque Anse Patates beach, this eco-friendly hotel offers comfortable rooms, a pool, and a beachside bar.

• **Le Nautique Luxury Waterfront Hotel:** This hotel offers luxurious waterfront rooms, a rooftop terrace, and premium dining experiences.

• **Six Senses Zil Pasyon:** Situated on the nearby private island of Felicite, this resort offers luxurious villas, a spa, a fitness center, and private beaches.

In conclusion, choosing where to stay in La Digue depends on your individual needs, preferences, and budget. Whether you prefer budget-friendly guesthouses or extravagant luxury resorts, La Digue has something for everyone. With its stunning beaches, crystal-clear waters, and idyllic surroundings, La Digue promises visitors a memorable and unforgettable stay.

Best hotels and resorts near La Digue's beaches

Here are some of the best hotels and resorts near La Digue's beaches, based on their amenities, location, and customer reviews.

1. Le Domaine de L'Orangeraie

Le Domaine de L'Orangeraie is a luxurious 5-star resort situated on a hill overlooking Anse Severe beach. The resort offers spacious villas designed to provide ultimate comfort and relaxation. Each villa has a private terrace with a Jacuzzi and an outdoor shower. The resort boasts modern facilities and amenities like a spa, fitness center, and a freshwater infinity pool. Dining options include two restaurants serving traditional Creole and International cuisines. The boutique hotel also arranges various activities, including beach picnics, snorkeling, scuba diving, and island excursions.

2. Patatran Village Hotel

Patatran Village Hotel is located on the western coast of La Digue Island, offering breathtaking views of the Indian Ocean from the private balconies of its unique bungalows. The eco-friendly resort is situated right on the Anse Patates beach, making it an ideal choice for beach enthusiasts. The resort features an outdoor pool, a restaurant serving local and international cuisine, and a beach bar that offers snacks and drinks. Patatran Village Hotel is also within reach of some of the island's other beautiful beaches, including Anse Source d'Argent, one of the most famous beaches in La Digue.

3. Château St Cloud

Château St Cloud is located on a hill with a stunning view of the ocean and sunset. The resort is surrounded by lush gardens, making it an ideal location for nature lovers. The resort features a range of rooms and suites with private terraces, most of which overlook the ocean. The hotel provides facilities such as an outdoor pool, a tennis court, a game room, a formal dining room, and a pool bar. Château St Cloud is also within walking distance of the Anse Réunion and Petite Anse beaches.

4. Le Relax Beach Resort

Le Relax Beach Resort is situated on Anse Reunion Beach, providing guests with lovely views of the turquoise waters. The resort is furnished with modern amenities and features spacious rooms with clean and sleek designs.

The resort also features an outdoor pool, a beachfront bar, and a restaurant serving local and international cuisines. Le Relax Beach Resort arranges visits to other beaches and excursions such as kayaking, snorkeling, and bike rentals.

5. Le Nautique Luxury Waterfront Hotel

Le Nautique Luxury Waterfront Hotel is located on the South West Coast of the Island adjacent to the Jetty. The boutique hotel provides stunning views of the ocean, and its location makes it convenient for exploring other beaches nearby. The hotel's elegant rooms feature modern conveniences such as flat-screen TVs and private balconies. Le Nautique offers facilities such as a rooftop terrace offering panoramic sea views, a spa, and a restaurant serving delicious cuisines, including premium seafood, and locally sourced ingredients.

In Conclusion,

Choosing the hotel or resort near your favorite beach can significantly impact your beach vacation experience, and La Digue's beautiful beaches have no shortage of impressive accommodations. The hotels listed above offer something unique and special depending on your preference, whether you're looking for eco-friendly, luxurious, family-friendly, or couples only resorts. No matter which one of these hotels you choose, you can always look forward to enjoying La Digue's stunning beaches and crystal-clear waters.

Where to Eat and Drink

Here is a comprehensive guide on where to eat and drink while on La Digue Island.

1. Fish Trap Restaurant

Fish Trap Restaurant is a popular dining spot on La Digue Island, known for serving up some of the best seafood on the island. Located in the heart of the La Passe village, Fish Trap Restaurant serves a variety of seafood dishes such as grilled octopus, shrimp in garlic butter, and crispy calamari. They also have vegetarian and meat options on their menu. The restaurant offers views of the harbor, situated next to the jetty, and is an excellent spot to enjoy a sunset meal.

2. Zerof Restaurant

Zerof Restaurant is located in a beautiful tropical garden setting and is a perfect place for intimate dining. The restaurant prides itself on using fresh and locally sourced ingredients to create their menu of Creole and International cuisines. Some of their specialties include curried octopus, grilled fish, and chicken tikka masala. They also offer vegetarian options and tasty desserts such as banoffee pie and pineapple carpaccio.

3. Chez Jules

Chez Jules is a beachfront restaurant situated on one of the most stunning beaches in the world, Anse Source d'Argent. This cozy restaurant serves delicious meals prepared with traditional Creole flavors like Creole fish curry, shark steak, and palm heart salad. The restaurant is also known for its cocktails and has a range of tropical drinks to choose from, including their signature drink, Coco Loco. Reservations are recommended as the restaurant can get crowded during peak hours.

4. Loutier Coco Bar

Loutier Coco Bar is a must-visit spot for anyone looking for a refreshing drink near the beach. The bar overlooks Anse Source d'Argent and is known for serving up cocktails with a tropical twist. Their signature drink, the Coco Loco, is a blend of fresh coconut water, local rum, and juice, served in a coconut shell and garnished with a slice of pineapple. If you're looking for non-alcoholic options, Loutier Coco Bar offers fresh juices and smoothies made with locally sourced fruits.

5. Snack Bellevue

Snack Bellevue is a charming Creole-style eatery situated on a hill overlooking the island's stunning scenery. They specialize in light meals like burgers, sandwiches, and wraps, making it an ideal spot for a quick lunch or snack. Their burgers and sandwiches are always freshly made and come with a choice of local vegetables and sauces. You can also grab a cold beer or soda to accompany your meal while enjoying the beautiful view.

In Conclusion,

La Digue Island is a food lover's paradise, with a broad range of dining options suited to fit different tastes and preferences. From beachfront restaurants to cozy garden settings or even roadside food vendors, there's something for everyone. The Island's cuisine is heavily influenced by its Creole roots, and the use of fresh seafood and locally sourced ingredients is evident in most dishes. If you're looking for an unforgettable culinary experience during your trip to La Digue Island, be sure to visit one of the establishments mentioned above and indulge in some of the best local delicacies and refreshing drinks the Island has to offer.

Local Creole Cuisine

Creole cuisine is a unique blend of flavors that originated in the Caribbean, particularly in the French-speaking islands. The cuisine is heavily influenced by French, African, and Caribbean flavors and techniques, resulting in a vibrant and tantalizing mix of dishes. The Seychelles, being one of the French-speaking islands, have a distinct Creole influence on their cuisine, which is evident in the local delicacies served up by various establishments on the Island.

The foundation of Seychellois cuisine is rice, often served with curries of fish, chicken, or vegetables. Coconut milk, chilies, and spices like ginger, garlic, and cinnamon all feature heavily in the preparation of these curries. Rice is sometimes replaced with other starches like cassava, sweet potato, or taro, and mashed potatoes are usually served on the side.

Seafood is undoubtedly the star of Seychellois cuisine, with fish like red snapper, kingfish, and tuna being the most commonly used. Octopus, squid, and crab are also popular seafood options. Fish is often cooked with spices and served with a side of salad or a vegetable curry.

One of the most famous Seychellois dishes is the bat curry, which is a spicy curry made with bat meat. Despite its reputation, bat curry is not widely available on the Island and is usually only found on special occasions such as weddings or festivals.

Another popular Seychellois dish is the la daube, which is a slow-cooked beef stew flavored with cinnamon, cloves, and coriander.

The dish is usually served with boiled cassava or rice.

Vegetarians also have a selection of dishes to choose from in Seychellois cuisine. The papaya chutney is a popular vegetarian side dish made with ripe papaya and a mix of spices, vinegar, and sugar. Palm heart salad is another delicious vegetarian option made with palm tree hearts, boiled and served with lettuce, carrots, and dressing.

Seychellois cuisine also includes a range of delicious snacks and desserts. The coconut cake is a sweet treat made with grated coconut, sugar, and flour. The breadfruit chips are a popular snack made with thinly sliced breadfruit, fried and flavored with salt and spices. Delimster is a local bread made with coconut milk, sugar, and flour, often served with tea or coffee.

In conclusion, Seychellois cuisine is a blend of French, African, and Caribbean influences, resulting in a unique and tantalizing mix of flavors. The cuisine is heavily focused on seafood, rice, and vegetables, along with a range of delicious snacks and desserts. Whether you're a fan of fish curries or vegetarian options, Seychellois cuisine offers something for everyone and is definitely worth trying on your next trip to the Island.

How to reach La Digue Island

If you're planning a trip to La Digue Island, it's essential to know how to reach there. This guide will provide you with detailed information on how to reach La Digue Island.

By Air

The first step in reaching La Digue Island is to fly to Seychelles. Seychelles International Airport (SEZ) is the main international airport and the gateway to the Seychelles. Once you land at the airport, you need to take a domestic flight to Praslin Island. Air Seychelles, the national airline, and other airlines like Cat Cocos offer flights from Mahe to Praslin Island. The flight is approximately 15-20 minutes. From Praslin Island, you need to take a ferry to La Digue Island.

By Ferry

La Digue Island is easily accessible by ferry from Praslin Island. The ferry ride takes around 20-30 minutes. There are two main ferry operators that run daily services between Praslin Island and La Digue Island - the Cat Cocos ferry and the Inter Island Ferry Seychelles. The Cat Cocos ferry is a high-speed catamaran and offers services from Baie Ste Anne on Praslin Island to La Passe on La Digue Island. The Inter Island Ferry Seychelles operates a slower ferry, offering services from the same locations. You can check the ferry schedules and fares online, and it's recommended to book your tickets in advance.

By Helicopter

For those who prefer a more luxurious and faster mode of transport, the helicopter is definitely an option. Zil Air is the premier helicopter tour and charter company in Seychelles, offering helicopter services between Mahe and La Digue Island. The helicopter ride is approximately 15 minutes and allows you to enjoy breathtaking views of the islands. It's essential to inquire about the cost of the helicopter ride as it's more expensive than the ferry.

Conclusion

Reaching La Digue Island is easy, whether you choose to travel by air, ferry, or helicopter. A combination of air and ferry is the most popular way to reach the Island. The ferry ride from Praslin Island to La Digue Island is the most common way of transportation. However, if you're looking for a more luxurious and faster mode of transport, the helicopter is an option. Remember to check the schedules and fares online and book your tickets in advance to avoid any delays or inconvenience.

Local Transportation options

Here's a detailed guide on the local transportation options in Seychelles.

Buses

Buses are the cheapest local transportation option in Seychelles, and they are operated by Seychelles Public Transport Corporation. The buses are equipped with air conditioning and usually, operate from 5 am to 8 pm. The buses are color-coded based on their routes, and the fares are based on the distance traveled. However, the buses are not always prompt and may sometimes be crowded.

Taxis

Taxis are a more comfortable and faster mode of transportation in Seychelles. Taxis can be found at the airport and around the main island of Mahe. The fares are fixed and regulated by the Seychelles government, and it's advisable to agree on the fare before starting the journey. Taxis can be a bit expensive if you plan to use them for long distances or for the entire day.

Rental Cars

Rental cars are the most convenient and popular mode of transportation in Seychelles, especially for tourists. Several car rental companies operate in Seychelles, mainly at the airport and on Mahe Island. The rental cars come in various models, and their prices vary depending on the type of car and the rental period. Driving is on the left side of the road in Seychelles, with some narrow and winding roads, so caution is advised. Valid driving licenses are required, and it is advisable to purchase an insurance policy that covers the rented vehicle.

Boat Excursions

Boat excursions are also a popular way of exploring the islands of Seychelles. Boat excursion operators offer various packages, including snorkeling, island tours, sunset cruises, and fishing trips. The boats depart from the main islands, and the costs depend on the duration and type of excursion.

Conclusion

Seychelles offers limited local transportation options, with buses, taxis, and rental cars being the main options. Buses are the cheapest option, while taxis are more comfortable and faster but can be expensive. Rental cars are the most convenient and popular option, but careful driving is recommended. Boat excursions are also available for exploring the islands. It is essential to choose the best transportation option based on convenience, comfort, and cost to have a pleasant traveling experience in Seychelles.

Tips for a Memorable Beach Vacation in La Digue

Are you planning a beach vacation in La Digue? With its pristine white sandy beaches, crystal-clear waters, and scenic landscapes, La Digue is the perfect destination for a relaxing and rejuvenating vacation. Here are some tips to help you make the most of your beach vacation in La Digue.

1. Choose the right time to go

The best time to go on a beach vacation in La Digue is between April and May or October and November when the weather is dry, and the crowds are low. During these months, you can enjoy the beaches with clear skies and pleasant temperatures. Avoid visiting during the rainy season from December to February when the island experiences heavy rainfall and strong winds.

2. Book your accommodations in advance

La Digue has a limited number of accommodations, and they tend to fill up quickly, especially during peak season. It is advisable to book your accommodations in advance to avoid any inconvenience. Choose a hotel or guesthouse that is close to the beach and offers amenities such as water sports, boat excursions, and spa facilities.

3. Pack appropriately

Pack light, comfortable clothing that is suitable for the beach, such as swimsuits, hats, sunglasses, and beachwear. Don't forget to pack sunscreen, insect repellent, and medication for any health conditions. If you plan to explore the island, wear comfortable shoes and carry a backpack with essentials like water, snacks, and a map.

4. Try local cuisine

La Digue offers a wide variety of local cuisines that are delicious and affordable. Try out the local seafood, curries, and other Creole delicacies at local restaurants or beachside food stalls. Don't forget to try the refreshing coconut water or freshly squeezed fruit juices.

5. Take a bike tour

La Digue is a small island, and the best way to explore it is by cycling. Rent a bicycle and take a tour of the island's scenic landscapes, stunning beaches, and quaint villages. Some of the popular attractions to visit on a bike tour include Anse Source d'Argent, Veuve Reserve, and the l'Union Estate.

6. Enjoy water sports

La Digue offers a variety of water sports and activities such as snorkeling, diving, kayaking, and fishing. These activities can be arranged by your hotel or by local tour operators. Explore the underwater world and discover the colorful marine life at various dive sites around the island.

Conclusion

La Digue is an ideal beach vacation destination, offering a perfect blend of relaxation, adventure, and natural beauty. By following these tips, you can make the most of your beach vacation and create unforgettable memories. Whether you're looking to lounge on the beach, explore the island's attractions, or indulge in water sports, La Digue has something for everyone.

What to pack

When it comes to packing for your beach vacation in La Digue, there are a few essential items that should be on your list. Whether you're planning to spend your days lounging on the beach, exploring the island's natural beauty, or indulging in water sports, here's what you should pack:

1. **Sunscreen** - The sun can be intense in La Digue, so it's important to protect your skin by wearing sunscreen. A high SPF sunscreen of at least 30 is recommended, and you should apply it regularly throughout the day.

2. **Swimsuits** - You'll likely be spending a lot of time on the beach or in the water, so be sure to pack plenty of swimsuits. It's also a good idea to bring a cover-up or sarong for when you want to take a break from the sun or head

to a beachside cafe for lunch.

3. Hat and sunglasses - To protect your eyes and face from the sun, bring a wide-brimmed hat and sunglasses. This will also help you stay comfortable when lounging on the beach or admiring the island's scenic landscapes.

4. Insect repellent - Mosquitoes and other insects can be a nuisance in La Digue, so be sure to pack insect repellent. You can also consider bringing long sleeves and pants to cover your skin during the evening.

5. First-aid kit - While La Digue is a safe and welcoming destination, it's always a good idea to be prepared with a basic first-aid kit. Include items such as band-aids, antiseptic wipes, pain relief medication, and any prescription medication you may need.

6. **Comfortable shoes** - While you'll likely be spending most of your time in flip flops or sandals, it's a good idea to bring comfortable walking shoes if you plan to explore the island's attractions or go on a bike tour.

7. **Water bottle** - Staying hydrated is crucial in La Digue's hot and humid climate. Bring a reusable water bottle to refill throughout the day and keep you refreshed as you explore the island.

8. **Backpack** - When heading out to explore, bring a backpack to carry any essentials such as water, snacks, sunscreen, and a map. This will also keep your hands free while biking or taking a walk.

In addition to these items, remember to pack any specific items you need for your planned activities. For example, if you plan to go snorkeling or diving, you'll need to bring your own equipment or rent it from a local provider. By packing smart and bringing everything you need for a comfortable and enjoyable vacation, you'll be able to make the most of your time in beautiful La Digue.

Safety tips

When planning a trip to any destination, safety should always be a top priority. The same applies when traveling to the beautiful island of La Digue in the Seychelles. While La Digue is a safe and welcoming destination, it's important to take precautions to ensure your safety while exploring the island. Here are some essential safety tips to keep in mind:

1. **Research the Area:** Before embarking on your journey to La Digue, do some research on the area you plan to visit. Familiarize yourself with the local customs, laws, and any potential risks. This knowledge can help you avoid dangerous situations and stay safe during your travels.

2. **Keep Your Valuables Secure:** When exploring La Digue, keep your valuables, such

as your passport, cash, and credit cards, secure. Use a money belt or a secure bag that you can keep close to your body at all times. Avoid carrying large amounts of cash or expensive jewelry that may draw unwanted attention to yourself.

3. **Be Cautious with Strangers:** While the majority of people you meet in La Digue are friendly and welcoming, exercise caution when interacting with strangers. Avoid giving out personal information and always trust your instincts when meeting new people.

4. **Stay Alert while Driving and Biking:** If you plan on renting a bike or driving a car on La Digue, be aware of the roads and traffic. Watch for pedestrians, other vehicles, and wildlife that may be crossing the road. Always wear a helmet while biking and follow local traffic laws.

5. Drink Responsibly: La Digue offers a variety of delicious cocktails and beers, but drinking responsibly is crucial to your safety. Don't drink and drive or operate a bike while under the influence of alcohol. Be aware of your surroundings and avoid walking alone at night.

6. Watch Out for Mosquitoes: Mosquitoes can be a nuisance in La Digue, and they can also transmit diseases like dengue fever and Zika virus. Use insect repellent, wear long sleeves and pants during the evening, and avoid staying in outdoor areas during peak mosquito hours, especially at dawn and dusk.

By following these safety tips, you can ensure a safe and enjoyable vacation on beautiful La Digue Island. Always be aware of your surroundings, keep your valuables secure, and take precautions to protect your health and safety. With proper planning and preparation, you can make the most of your trip and create unforgettable memories in this stunning destination.

Sustainable tourism practices

Sustainable tourism practices are becoming increasingly popular as travelers become more conscious of the impact they have on the environment and local communities. Sustainable tourism refers to travel that preserves the environment, promotes economic prosperity, and benefits local communities.

There are several key principles of sustainable tourism that travelers and tourism businesses should adhere to. The first principle is to minimize the impact of tourism on the environment. This can be done by reducing waste, conserving resources, and promoting eco-friendly practices such as recycling, energy conservation, and sustainable water management.

The second principle is to support the local economy. This involves supporting locally-owned businesses, sourcing local products and services, and ensuring that tourism revenue benefits the local community. By doing so, sustainable tourism can help to create jobs, encourage economic growth, and promote cultural exchange.

The third principle of sustainable tourism is to promote cultural awareness and respect for local communities. This involves educating travelers about local customs, traditions, and history, and promoting cultural exchange. Travelers should also be mindful of their behavior when interacting with local communities, being respectful and considerate at all times.

Finally, sustainable tourism practices should support the preservation of natural and cultural heritage. This can involve supporting conservation efforts, protecting wildlife and wilderness areas, and promoting the preservation of historical and cultural sites.

There are several benefits to sustainable tourism practices. By minimizing the impact of tourism on the environment, sustainable tourism can help to preserve natural resources for future generations. Similarly, by supporting the local economy and promoting cultural exchange, sustainable tourism can help to build stronger, more resilient communities.

There are also benefits for tourism businesses that adopt sustainable practices. By being environmentally responsible, businesses can reduce costs, improve their reputation, and attract eco-conscious travelers. Sourcing local products and services can also help businesses to reduce costs and differentiate themselves in a competitive market.

In conclusion, sustainable tourism practices are essential for protecting the environment, supporting local communities, and preserving cultural heritage. By adopting sustainable practices, both travelers and tourism businesses can contribute to a more responsible and sustainable tourism industry, one that benefits everyone involved.

Conclusion

In conclusion, La Digue is a stunning destination that offers an idyllic tropical getaway for beach enthusiasts. With its crystal -clear waters, lush vegetation, and white sandy beaches, La Digue is an ideal place to unwind and relax. However, as with any travel destination, it's essential to take safety precautions to ensure a smooth and enjoyable trip.

When visiting La Digue, it's important to be aware of your surroundings and mindful of any potential dangers. By doing your research ahead of time and keeping your valuables secure while exploring the island, you can minimize the risk of theft or other security concerns.

If you plan on driving or biking, it's crucial to exercise caution on the roads, which can be narrow and winding. Additionally, it's essential to stay alert while enjoying sun, fun, and activities like swimming, snorkeling, or diving.

To have the best experience in La Digue, it's also important to respect the culture and traditions of the Seychelles. Make sure to adhere to dress codes and be mindful of local customs. And, if you're in doubt, always ask a local for advice or recommendations.

In summary, La Digue provides a magical holiday destination for beach lovers, and it's a place where you can relax, rejuvenate, and reconnect with nature. By taking the necessary precautions, you can stay safe and make the most of your time on this beautiful island in the Seychelles. Whether you're exploring hidden coves or soaking up the sun on a secluded beach, La Digue is a place where you can create unforgettable memories that will last a lifetime. So, pack your bags, explore La Digue, and immerse yourself in paradise.